HIJABI ABC'S

WRITTEN BY NORA MOHTADI

DEDICATED TO ALL THE STRONG, INDEPENDENT,
AND CONFIDENT GIRLS AROUND THE WORLD
WHO ARE JUST LIKE MY MISK.

A HIJABI IS.....

Always aspiring
to be amazing

Beautiful Inside and Out

Cultivating Creativity

DARING TO SHINE BRIGHT

Effortlessly
Brave

Friendly to All

Grateful for her blessings

HELPING THOSE IN NEED

Inspiring Others

JUST HAVING FUN

KIND TO ALL

LOVING DAUGHTER, MOTHER, SISTER, WIFE

Making Things Happen

NEVER BACKING
DOWN

Overcoming Every Obstacle

POSITIVELY PEACEFULL

QUITE LIKE NO
OTHER

Radiantly Respectful

STUNNINGLY SELF-CONFIDENT

TRUE TO HER WORD

Uplifting Those Around Her

VIBRANTLY VALUABLE

WISE BEYOND
HER YEARS

Xenial Host

Yes Queen!

ZESTFUL AND EXUBERANT